THE LAST DREAM

(A Search For God)

Samuel Alesich

BALBOA. PRESS
A DIVISION OF HAY HOUSE

Copyright © 2011 Samuel Alesich

All rights reserved. No part of this book may be used or reproduced by any means, graphic, electronic, or mechanical, including photocopying, recording, taping or by any information storage retrieval system without the written permission of the publisher except in the case of brief quotations embodied in critical articles and reviews.

Balboa Press books may be ordered through booksellers or by contacting:

Balboa Press
A Division of Hay House
1663 Liberty Drive
Bloomington, IN 47403
www.balboapress.com
1-(877) 407-4847

Because of the dynamic nature of the Internet, any web addresses or links contained in this book may have changed since publication and may no longer be valid. The views expressed in this work are solely those of the author and do not necessarily reflect the views of the publisher, and the publisher hereby disclaims any responsibility for them.

The author of this book does not dispense medical advice or prescribe the use of any technique as a form of treatment for physical, emotional, or medical problems without the advice of a physician, either directly or indirectly. The intent of the author is only to offer information of a general nature to help you in your quest for emotional and spiritual well-being. In the event you use any of the information in this book for yourself, which is your constitutional right, the author and the publisher assume no responsibility for your actions.

Any people depicted in stock imagery provided by Thinkstock are models, and such images are being used for illustrative purposes only.
Certain stock imagery © Thinkstock.

ISBN: 978-1-4525-3269-1 (sc)
ISBN: 978-1-4525-3270-7 (e)

Library of Congress Control Number: 2011902409

Printed in the United States of America

Balboa Press rev. date: 2/11/2011

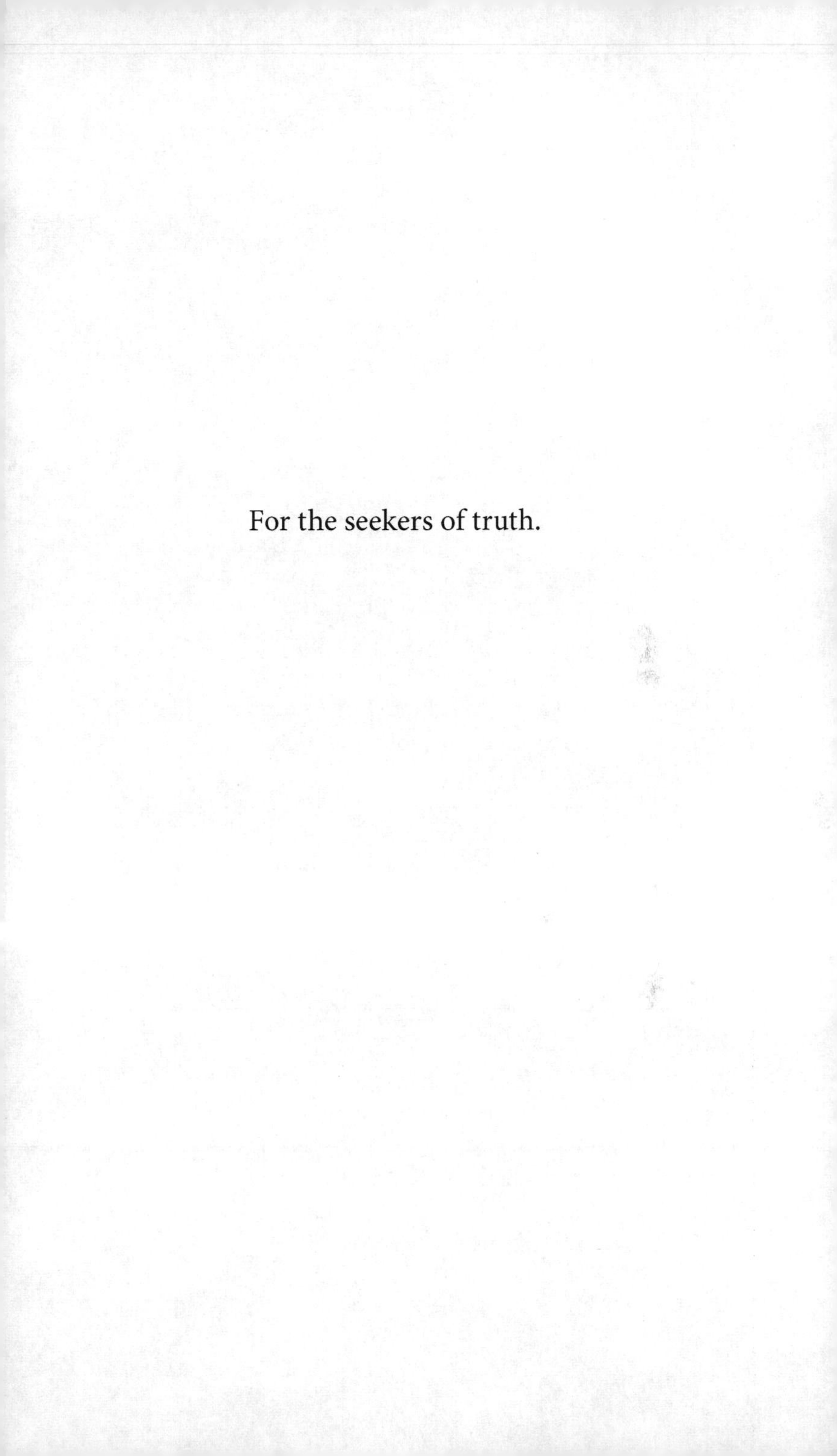

For the seekers of truth.

"I can do all things through the Christ Presence within me."

--- Saint Paul

"For behold, the Kingdom of God is within you."

--- Luke 17:21

"And He departed from our sight that we might return to our heart, and there find Him. For He departed, and behold, He is here."

---St. Augustine

"Know ye not that ye are the temple of God . . . that your body is the temple . . . Of the Living God."

--- Corinthian's 16:19

"There is only one path which goes inward, where you will not find a single human being. Where you will only find silence, peace."

--- Osho

TABLE OF CONTENTS

SANTA FE, NEW MEXICO

One January day, I walked down a street in Santa Fe, New Mexico, as large snow flakes swirled to the ground. Bells were ringing in the towers of St. Francis Cathedral, a deep, clear sound heard in the winding streets and surrounding mountains. In the cathedral, I sat in a pew and stared at candle flames, golden and flickering as though fanned by some spiritual hand. Light streamed in through long, and multi-colored panes of glass, and I followed them upward to a majestic ceiling. I felt small and humble and, yes, honored to be there. After a while a choir began to sing, their beautiful young voices reverberating off the walls--and I felt at the time that surely they were heard all over the city. It was easy to believe in God.

TRAGEDY IN MEXICO CITY

Sometime in late September of 1968, I rode a bus out of New Orleans to San Antonio, Texas, where the World Fair was being held. After several days, I made my way down to Monterey, Mexico, and its beautiful mountains surrounding the city. Days later, I boarded a bus for the long ride to Mexico City. One of my reasons for going there was my desire to visit the Museum of Anthropology, which had opened four years earlier.

My timing for a visit to Mexico City was terrible for two reasons, one of which was the opening of the Olympic Games on October 12th, meaning that I had only several days to visit before having to vacate the city because all hotel rooms had been booked far in advance.

The second reason my timing was so bad was because on October 2, 1968, an estimated three hundred people, most of them students, were killed for protesting the use of funds for staging the games, rather than using those funds for social programs. They died in a hail of bullets fired by the Mexican Army. Over a thousand people were injured.

The bus made many stops across the vast and arid Mexican landscape. For many hours, I listened to the dull roar of the engine and a slight clicking sound from the tires against the roadway. I felt sad for the people who lived in the huts we passed, without electricity or running water.

It was growing quite dark as we approached Mexico City. Suddenly, to my great surprise and delight, I spotted a huge illuminated cross placed high on a mountain top. As I stared at this beautiful cross floating against a cloudless night sky, my spirits lifted. I became filled with a quiet joy. I felt a deep love for everyone and everything.

The following day, after leaving the Museum of Anthropology in Chapultepec Park, I walked along Reforma Avenue. Reforma is a grand tree-lined street that has many spectacular monuments. I encountered dozens of military trucks, filled with soldiers, going every which way in the city. I felt that the troop transports were very much out of place; a feeling which tempered greatly the enjoyment I had experienced all that day.

That afternoon, I climbed the stairs to my fourth floor room, tired and disturbed by what I had seen. That night, I lay in darkness and listened for hours to an endless wail of sirens in the city. In streets that lay in the shadow of that towering cross high up on the mountain, human beings were dying. In this very religious country, unarmed women and men were being shot to death. And I asked, "Why God?'

INSIGHT TO A HURRICANES PATH

While employed by a large oil company in the Gulf of Mexico off the Louisiana coast, I had many times assisted with shutting in oil and gas production platforms because of approaching hurricanes.

One year after completing what was required for protecting against an approaching hurricane, I called my wife to tell her that within hours I would be driving home to Northeast Louisiana. She immediately asked what my mother and father's evacuation plan was. They lived some seventy miles below New Orleans behind a high levee that not only kept the Mississippi River out, but also the sea. A place where I grew up and which I knew to be many feet below sea level.

I told my wife that Mother and Father would be staying at a large school just outside of New Orleans that was used as a shelter. Father did not drive, and he would not ride the three hundred plus miles to where I lived. My wife immediately became alarmed at my words.

"No," she all but shouted. 'They must not stay there. The school will not be a safe place." I knew that she often had premonitions of coming events, and that she loved my parents, so she was concerned for their safety. I told her not to worry; the school was the same large brick school that we, ourselves, had taken shelter in several times during past storms when we had lived only a mile from my parents.

The reminder of the strength of that school house calmed her, but I wanted to ease her concerns further.

"Besides," I told her, "the storm's projected path will bring it across Florida into the Atlantic Ocean."

She immediately blurted out. "It's going to come back. It's going to stop and come back and strike the Louisiana coast."

It's what she felt at the time, and she always said whatever she felt strongly about without thought as to where it came from or if it sounded reasonable or not. These premonitions always arose when an impending situation threatened in some way those whom she cared deeply for.

Many hours later, while the storm was positioned over Florida and moving east, it stalled. It's foremost outer bands to the east were in the Atlantic Ocean; to the west, they were in the Gulf of Mexico. When I heard that the storm had stalled, I had no doubt what-so-ever that it would return to strike Louisiana, and it did. Many hours later, it slammed into the Louisiana coast just east of new Orleans, tearing the roof off a school house that was being used as a shelter. No one was hurt.

And no, it was not the school house my mother and father were in, some twenty miles away. And yet, amazingly, my wife had been so on target with her warning. I was not overly surprised. Our subconscious mind, our life force, that all-knowing God-Presence that resides in each one of us made known to my wife the destructive path of the storm. Evidently, at the time my wife tuned in, there were either atmospheric or oceanic conditions either existing or building that would determine the path of the storm, in spite of what weather satellites and our best meteorologist believed to be true.

But I was puzzled. How could this great intelligence that resides within each one of us know that this hurricane would damage a school, thus enabling my wife who had tuned in, to feel that a brick school building was not a safe shelter. Days later, I had my answer. Television and newspapers informed the public that the school board intended to sue the school's building contractors. The school's structural short comings were known to its builders. Since it was known in the minds of the builders, it was a part of universal knowledge: information that is available to all of us who are able to tap into it.

So---. Who knew the destructive path of this storm? Who was watching? God was. And the element that makes one aware of God's Presence in their life, is love. The love that my wife held for my mother and father enabled her to have insight to an unfolding event.

CHILD LOST IN A SWAMP

There was a story in a newspaper of a ten-year-old autistic boy who became lost in a swamp for four days and nights. The same swamp which had claimed the lives of four army rangers due to hypothermia while training one year earlier.

One thing the boy had going for him was that he was an excellent swimmer. Although the swamp is practically impassable and heavily infested with snakes and alligators, he managed to traverse fourteen miles without food or clean water.

Bad thunderstorms with much lightning during the nights had been one of rescue workers' many concerns. When asked if she was deeply concerned about the lightning, the mother replied. 'Do you really think God would strike this child with lightning? Wouldn't that be redundant?'

When found, the boy was stark naked and covered with cuts and bruises. He was also very hungry.

His mother was willing to live with the notion of a miracle. “I guess God was looking for something to do,” she said. “I guess He looked down and said, “Lets fix things up a little bit.”

FALLING STARS

Following hurricane Katrina's strike on the Gulf Coast of the United States in August 2005, well over three million people had no electricity. Somewhere near a quarter of a million had no homes.

In the weeks following the great storm, people slept in tents or in automobiles or without bedding upon the ground after moving aside a mountain of debris. It was terribly hot. It was very easy to cry.

Without the glare from incandescent lighting, the night sky looked incredibly beautiful. Millions of points of light gently falling downward, so that one was filled with wonder. Someone said that it was as though God was everywhere.

Then, from across the stricken land, a hot and sticky wind would touch your skin, bringing with it the stench of death. Once again, a sadness would settle upon you like the blanket of stars.

THE SAFETY OF A CHILD

Once, while watching the evening news, I heard about a tornado that had completely destroyed a house. Hours later, rescuers found a baby lodged high up in a tree. The baby was unharmed.

A family's daily blanket of love, of prayer for their loved one's safety, for his or her well being, will help insulate them from harm.

"God is with my family, and all is well." And use their name. And remember to say this every day so that it becomes a mantra. And believe it to be a truth in your life and in the life of the ones you love and pray for. It may seem simple, and yet it is so powerful. It is not asking for anything. It is a statement recognizing and acknowledging that God is the power. If you are asking for someone's safety, then you miss. You don't have to get permission. God's Presence within you gives you what you believe to be true.

TRAGEDY ON A GREAT RIVER

One summer, on a bank of the Mississippi River below New Orleans, a great tragedy occurred. A mother and her three young children had stopped to visit a pre-Civil War fort. They had traveled from west of New Orleans to pick up the children's father who was a captain on a large crew boat that serviced oil rigs in the open waters of the Gulf of Mexico.

They were early, so the mother gave in to her two boys pleading to play on the sand bars along the water's edge as other children were doing. One of the boys went out too far and he began to struggle against the pull of the strong current. His brother went out to help him and found that the river bank had fallen away. He attempted to return to the shore, but he could not break free of the strong current.

Their mother, realizing that her two boys were drowning, went out to try to save them. All three of them drowned in the dirty water of that river while the young girl stood on the river bank and screamed for someone to help her family.

Later, a sheriff deputy took the young girl to the boat dock and told her father that he had lost his wife and two sons in the same river that he worked on.

I had often parked my automobile at this same beach and walked along the water's edge. Large ships from countries around the world ply their way upriver towards New Orleans, seventy miles away. There is most often a wind from off the water and a sound of breaking waves against the hard-packed sand of the beach.

Several hours after this great tragedy occurred, I listened to the news account on the 6:00 pm news. I was filled with sadness and much anger. The often spoken words that "God has his reasons" rang hollow. I don't believe anyone would have wanted to mention to the father of those two boys that "God will not give you more than you can bear."

MEMORY OF A FRIEND WHO DIED IN VIETNAM

It was wonderful growing up next to a great river and the seemingly endless miles of river levee below New Orleans. The two-mile wide strip of land sandwiched between earthen levees nurtured many thousands of citrus trees.

We lived in a two-room shack without electricity. We caught rain water in fifty-five gallon oil drums and used an outhouse out back.

People threw their garbage on the outside of the river levee. Once Christmas had passed, my brother and I would comb the garbage dumps for a Christmas tree. There most always were several to choose from. We picked up broken bulbs and silver-colored icicles and ribbons and bows to decorate the tree. Even though we knew that Mother would not allow us to bring the tree into the house, we drew comfort from the fact that we had one.

I must have been fourteen years old when we received our first Christmas tree, brought to us by a friend of our family after his school class had finished their Christmas party and broke for the holidays. Six years later, he was killed in that senseless and unnecessary war in Vietnam, along with more than fifty-eight thousand other young men.

A short time following the firing of the rifles and the folding of the flag, I walked alone on the river levee. On my left, I could see the brown water of the river and two ships as they made their way against the current toward New Orleans. On my right, I saw the tall, white Catholic Church, Our Lady Of Good Harbor, and the white tombs of the graveyard where I had watched the burial of my friend. The same large church where as a kid I had sat so many Sundays on hard wooden pews and listened for the tolling of the great bells. Where I had watched sunlight streaming in through tall, multi-colored stained glass windows; and statues of Saints looked down on Gods gathered flock. Filled with wonder, I had also felt incredibly small in that large, Cavernous house of God - - but I never once felt alone.

Now, as I looked at the church and the graveyard beyond, I felt very much alone. For the second time in a short while, my eyes filled with tears. I remembered the time my friend had come to our door with our first Christmas tree. I thought of how needless that war was that took his life. I felt that God could have prevented that war - - that He was a do-nothing God. It was one of the saddest days of my life.

A FRIEND'S TRIP HOME

I worked four years as a Security Officer at a large casino on the Mississippi Gulf Coast. I made friends with a cab driver named Steve, whom I often talked with while on duty in Valet Parking. After not seeing him for over a week, upon his return, I asked him if he had been sick. What he told me is a remarkable story.

Steve had been parked outside the casino along with several other cabs when a gentleman approached him and asked if my friend could drive him to Denver Colorado, a distance of some fourteen hundred miles. This was two weeks following 9-11 and he didn't want to fly.

My friend was greatly surprised. He had grown up in Denver. He told the man that it would cost him a lot of money, and that he would have to be provided a room and meals. The gentleman told him that the cost was not a problem. The cost for the cab and his service and the room and meals would be provided. The man left for a short time and returned with his luggage. He counted out the fifteen hundred dollars that Steve requested and they began their trip.

An hour outside of Denver, Steve called and surprised his mother, telling her he was almost home. He spent two wonderful days with her. On his return trip to the Gulf Coast, he stopped at his son's house in Texas, and that day was his son's birthday.

For some time, Steve had held a deep desire to visit his mother, to return home, but he did not have the money to enable him to do so. Far more that a desire, it was a deep longing, a hunger, that felt like a hurting inside. He told me that for several days, he could not get the thought of Mother and home out of his mind. He had resolved that he would have to save enough money to make the trip.

What I wish to share is that his deep longing, his love, if you will--was embraced by his subconscious mind, and that God Presence which lies awake within all of us moved for him. God moved, and brought about the conditions that allowed him to go home.

AN OLD DOG NAMED TITO

Everyone who had ever seen the old dog swore that he was crazy. He would often nip at the heels of an elderly gentleman named Mr. Miller as he walked along the river road, seventy miles below New Orleans on his way to a large Catholic Church. The dog belonged to an old Yugoslavian who had named him Tito, after the long-time leader of Yugoslavia.

One day, Tito bit Mr. Miller, and the following day, the old man carried a gun down to the highway and shot the dog through his hind leg. Of course, Tito didn't die. He gave Mr. Miller a little more space, probably intending to do so only until his leg healed.

Shortly thereafter, a major hurricane named Betsy struck New Orleans and that long peninsula south of the city that juts into the Gulf of Mexico. I remember looking out a window and watching seventy-foot long light poles being blown over in a school yard a quarter of a mile away. About that time, my father decided that the family should abandon our house and go next door to a much larger one that stood a good five feet off of the ground. My father and I held the hands of my younger brother, my sister, and my mother as we ran along the base of the levee.

Night came and the one-hundred-fifty mile an hour winds pushed the water of the Gulf over the top of the river levee directly behind the house. Daylight revealed that water from the Gulf of Mexico covered all of the land. Our house lay broken and sitting in four feet of water.

The highway was under water, and we walked upon it to survey damage to other people's property. There was debris everywhere, and dead cattle that had been swept across the river from pastures on the east bank of the Mississippi River. There were dead people, too, but we didn't know that at the time. A mile south of where we lived, most of the houses had water to their roof tops.

Mr. Miller's house was damaged beyond repair and sitting in five feet of water. The old man was sitting in a rocking chair on what remained of a porch, and that old dog named Tito sat quietly beside him. They had made their peace at last.

I included this story because I like it. It's a feel-good story. I have wondered...what if the old gentleman had brought a bone to Tito the first time the dog had challenged him. Perhaps a single saltine cracker would have brought about a friendship, and so much anger and pain could have been avoided. Love is always the answer. Saint Francis once said, "Where there is hatred, let me sow love."

HURRICANE CAMILLE

Shortly before making landfall on August 17, 1969, hurricane Camille reached a sustained wind speed of 190 miles an hour. As the powerful storm approached I lay in a deep sleep in a trailer house seventy miles below New Orleans.

Hours earlier, myself and others had spent most of the day shutting in oil producing wells in the Gulf of Mexico. Returning to the trailer house, I sat eating a sandwich as a police car drove trough the park, it's hauntingly beautiful blue lights flashing and it's public addresse system announcing an immediate evacuation.

On the table in front of me was my large, Remington Noiseless typewriter. Ordered from a Montgomery Ward catalog, it was my most prized possesion. A western novel that I had finished writing lay on the table beside it. As did my camera along with pictures taken at the Worlds Fare in San Antonio Texas one year earlier. There were also pictures that I had taken in Mexico City.

I knew that I should pack my belongings, get a move on. I stood up and suddenly realized that I was bone tired. I knew that the single roadway out would be crowded with evacuees and that the going would be slow for some time. I walked into the bedroom, removed my shoes and fell into a deep sleep.

Sometime into the night I was awakened with a terribly overpowering feeling of dread. An inner voice was repeating over and over again. "Get out! Get out! Get out!"

I was aware that the trailer was shaking by the force of a strong wind. Torrential rain pounded against the windows and the thin aluminumn siding.

As I hurriedly put my shoes on the voice never let up. "Get out! Get out!" I picked up my wallet and my automobile keys and hurried into the living room with the intention of packing my belongings. Just then a hard gust shook the trailer violently as the wind howled. The voice was screaming into my head now. "Get out!" I trembled as a current of fear ran through my body. I ran to the door and locked it behind me.

The wind slammed me against my automobile, but I pushed off and made my way to the drivers side. I owned an old automobile that had many miles on it. As I inserted the key into the ignition switch, I prayed. "Please God, let it start." And it did.

As I drove out of the completely deserted trailer park, the strong wind slammed into the automobile again and again. I held tightly onto the wheel, leaning forward to peer out of a windshield that was being pounded by sheets of rain. The windshield wipers moved frantically, adding to the noise. "Please God, let me not have stayed too long," I prayed.

Moments later I turned onto the highway leading to New Orleans. I saw no one else on the highway. I stepped heavily upon the accelerator and the big automobile quickly gained speed. The trees alongside the roadway were whipping wildly and small branches and leaves flew across my path and struck the side of the automobile with a thud. I was surprised to see that there was still electricity. That the power poles had not yet blown down. At that moment I realized that God was there for me. I had been awakened from a deep sleep and provided a way out, even to the lighting. "Thank You, God."

I joined my mother and father and my brother in a large school house outside of New Orleans. Sometimes later we were informed that everything in that lower pensisula from which I had escaped, was lost. The gulf waters had easily topped the twenty-eight foot high earthen levee. There was nothing left of the trailer park where I had lived. Nothing much left of anything.

For years I had prayed that God would always be there to protect me. That I would be warned of any impending danger. That God Presence has never failed me.

HURRICANE KATRINA AFTERMATH

For weeks following hurricane Katrina in August 2005, the heat was almost unbearable. I live thirty miles north of the Mississippi Gulf Coast, far from the thirty-to-forty foot high wall of water that swept as far as six miles inland.

The entire roof of the small diner that my wife operated was blown off during the height of the storm, and the twelve-foot-high ceiling fell in on my mother, sister, wife and me. None of us were physically hurt.

This storm was not a new experience for my eighty-two year old mother. In September of 1965, our family narrowly escaped from a house below New Orleans when hurricane Betsy pushed a wall of water over the river levee and broke our house in half. In Katrina, both my mother and my sister lost their home.

In the aftermath of Katrina, there was no electricity, or running water. No cell phones or land line service. No grocery stores. No gasoline.

In the first weeks following the great storm, it was as though nothing lived. There were no birds seen or heard in the trees. No squirrels or rabbits. Nothing but an east wind that blew constantly through the stripped trees, carrying the stench of death. The sky was clear at night, and in the pitch darkness, the stars never looked brighter.

I had over a hundred trees blown down. In my back yard, one could not walk twenty feet without crawling over a tree trunk or broken branches.

There were days when I worked angrily from daylight to dark cutting trees and raking every foot of the yard with a pitchfork to pick up a sea of sticks to burn. My largest tree, a great white oak lay on its side at the bottom of the hill. I had often laid my hands on its massive, towering trunk and talked to it. Now, at least once a day, I took a break from work and sat on a large Tulip Poplar that lay alongside the oak and talked to it until I felt that all of the life force had left it.

I told my great oak that I was sorry. That several million trees had fallen. Property damage was said to surpass eighty-one billion dollars. An estimated three million people had lost electricity. That perhaps as many as a quarter of a million people had either loss their homes or had them severely damaged. Two thousand people had died. That God was in control of nothing. That it was all the fault of global warming.

And yes, I am grateful to be alive. There are stories of people who lived near the beach who survived by clinging to the upper branches of oak trees after their homes had broken into pieces. A lot of people have suffered terribly. Suicide rates are high, even three years later. Along with being thankful, there is great pain.

In the weeks, months, and years following the great storm, an endless stream of volunteers from churches all across the country converged on the Gulf Coast. A great blessing to the beleaguered people. There is a lot of love in a lot of people's hearts. The love that was and is the Christ Jesus is alive in a lot of peoples hearts.

NOTHING IS EVER LOST

I once spent six hours in a class taught by the psychic and medium, John Holland. There were perhaps sixty people in the class, and we did many exercises.

At one point, I placed both palms of my hands several inches from a young woman's head as she sat in a straight-backed chair. I had never seen this woman before, and I was not told her name. She had been instructed to think of the worst experience in her life. I closed my eyes and immediately sensed a great blackness. A blackness far greater than what one would normally experience when closing one's eyes. Without thinking of saying it, without a mental picture, I blurted out, "You were involved in a terrible automobile accident."

And she immediately replied, "No, not me, but my best friend was killed in an automobile accident." This took no longer than perhaps three or four seconds and is recognized as "intuitive knowing."

Nothing is ever lost. Depak Chopra once said, "All the struggle to learn, when all we have to do is remember."

In her book entitled, 'Channeling,' [1] Kathryn Ridall tells of her experience with Spirit Guides. On the first page of her book she explains:

"Ultimately we can never know for sure whether channeling is a fabrication of our own minds, or true communication with other beings. But the way I look at it, if we have invented all these channelings, the human mind has an amazing capacity to access wisdom far beyond our conscious knowledge. And if we have not made it up, then the universe is full of many wise beings who love us and want to help us.

Pick your Miracle."

Our subconscious mind - that God Presence within us that knows everything that has ever befallen the human race - never sleeps.

1 Bantam Books March 1988

RWANDA GENOCIDE
(THE WORLD WATCHED!)

The United Nations list the death toll during the 1994 Rawandha Genocide to be 800,000. Machetes were used to hack to death the men, women and children of the Tutsis tribe.

In one incident, more than 1,500 Tutsis sought refuge in a Catholic Church. Members of the Hutu tribe used a bulldozer to knock down the church and proceeded to methodically hack all of its inhabitants to death.

The world watched and did nothing.

ERIN & STEVE (PART OF MY DREAM)

Erin and Steve are seated on a blanket on top of a sand dune overlooking the sea. The wind is from the sea and it is cool against their skin. There is a sound of waves breaking in the shallows, and from time to time, the sharp cry of a seagull.

"You know, Erin, geologists tell us that once there was no Atlantic ocean. Europe and Africa were one with North and South America. One super continent. The Appalachian Mountains at that time were higher than the Himalayans, higher than Mount Everest. Systemic activity split the land mass. As the continents began to move apart, some two hundred millions years ago, the Atlantic Ocean was formed.

"Where was God, back then, Erin? Man was not on the earth at that time, was he? Surely it would not have taken man millions of years to crawl out of a cave and build a fire. If man was here, than the question that begs

-- did God create him stupid? If man was not here at that time, then what was God waiting for?"

Erin smiled and nodded her head several times. "The great mystery, right Steve?" She did not wait for a reply.

"The word, 'why,' is often used when talking about God. Why does God allow so many terrible things to happen? And yet, God is here," she said, looking up to hold Steve's eyes.

"And we are God, are we not? Created in His image. We are the creators. At least co-creators. Our every thought is creative. The God Presence within us brings into reality that which we dwell upon, whether consciously or unconsciously. Our innermost desires, our feelings, are acted upon, even if we are not consciously aware of them. Negative thoughts. . . and even suppressed feelings of anger, or guilt - - bring about all manner of disease. It's not that a God off somewhere decides, we decide.

"Man did evolve, Steve. Man, not our Spirit, which is God. Spirit always was, always will be. Man evolved from the lowest life forms, and then the Holy Spirit came, God came. God does not reason. God knows nothing about ego, about jealousy or anger or greed or hatred. There's just God. Just energy. Just vibration.

Just light. Just love. Just is. Always has been. Always will be.

"God, our creator, fulfills our deepest desires. If they be good or bad. That which we embrace we bring into our presence. We create the conditions that become our reality. There are no accidents.

"Steve, the chatter in our mind never stops. Even when we try to meditate, to be still, our thoughts continue to bombard us. Oh, perhaps there are a few people who can still the noise. But for myself, I can do so for only moments.

"Positive thoughts will bring a blessing into our life. On the other hand, thoughts of anger or feelings of hatred toward others, or directed towards ourselves for some wrong that we feel we have done, will bring misfortune, accidents, and yes even disease to our bodies.

"And yes, I realize that I'm repeating myself. It's just that I feel very strongly about this living Presence of God within us. Even if we are not consciously aware of negative thoughts; regardless, if we harbor them day in and day out, then that is what we will attract as our reality. God does not choose for us, we choose. God's Presence gives to us our most heartfelt desires.

A NEW DAWN

I awaken with the light of morning streaming through my bedroom window in the back of the house. The colors of the sky above a green field are bright-red, orange and gold. There is a great stillness.

On the wall beyond the foot of the bed is a poster of a large gold-colored bird soaring skyward into the orange and gold of a newborn day. The caption beneath the picture reads . . . "It is time to wake up again and remember who you really are." And who I really am, and who you really are, is God. Not I, Samuel Alesich. Not this body, but the life force, the intelligence, the God Presence that lives within me and protects me and brings into my life the fruits of my desire, and yes, my dreams. God, that creative Presence that brings to me (for better or worse), that which I mentally entertain all day long.

I and my Father are one.

VANESSA (A CHILD OF MY IMAGINATION)

A young woman named Vanessa is seated on the exposed roots of a large tree beside a great river. Brown water swirls over the clay bank and over the fingers of red roots making a gurgling sound.

She looks up, and a cool autumn breeze from off the river caresses her face and she smiles.

There are many willow trees, and their trailing green, leafy branches offer shelter from a hot sun set in a clear sky

She closes her eyes, and once again, she is aware of the coolness and the stirring of her long blonde hair against her forehead.

Now, something in the wind calls her name. "Vanessa." Softly, wistfully. And again, "Vanessa."

But how could the wind know her name...unless it was God speaking?

She had often played a "What If?" game. What if there was no wind? What if there were no trees. No rivers to run to the sea. No oceans. No flowers. No love. No hope. What if there was no God?

"But there is a God," she thought. "Only moments ago, He whispered my name. He said, "I love you."

"But he did not, Vanessa," she rebuked herself. "What was whispered to you was only your name. There was nothing about love. Nothing that suggested God. It was only your imagination."

"But I could find God," she thought. "If I could take a boat and journey down this river to the sea. - - I would find a small island there. There would be a sand beach, and shore birds, and at night, Ghost Crabs scurrying from one burrow to another. Rabbits and raccoons would live among the sea oats and bayberry shrubs that grow profusely on top of the large sand dunes.

"In the forest behind the dunes, there would be deer. Sometimes I will watch them when they come to drink at the fresh water pond. All day, I would hear the cry of birds, and at night, I would listen to the thundering roar of huge waves as they broke in the shallows thirty-yards out from the beach.

"I would watch moonlight shimmer silver on the water as it rolled ashore in a display of bubbles and white foam. At times, I would observe a large sea turtle as she crawled from the sea to lay her eggs in the warm sand high on the beach. God most definitely would be there with me, alone on my island.

"But where were the people?" Well - - she didn't need them. She could be an island onto herself. "But you cannot be, Vanessa." Then what is it that makes this island such a perfect place? And now she knew that it was love. Love for all of the life on the island, and yes, for the very island itself.

And if there were people on the island, could she not love them also? Now she felt sad, because people often fought with one another. Still, if they could remember to love one another, at least some of the time, then there was hope.

If love dies, then hope for the human race dies. God dies. Human beings did often love one another. And yet they often fought and killed one another. What if there were another world war. She closed her eyes and remembered a short story that she had once read titled, "The Last Flower."

THE LAST FLOWER

When Mary regained consciousness, the wind that blew from the top of the mountain felt cool on the burns on her face and arms. The air was filled with the stench of burnt flesh. It was the second day after the bomb.

The war was over. All the soldiers were gone. All the flowers were gone, but the dead were everywhere, just beyond the mountain.

She thought that she would stand, and was surprised to find she could not move her legs. She recalled now that she had been walking in her father's pasture a hundred yards from their home when she had seen the terrible fire in the sky - - and she had known.

She had run toward the house, but the tremendous wind had blown her down time and again; and later, she had let the wind take her beyond the hill so that she would not have to look toward home again.

Looking about her now, she saw that what little grass remained was badly scorched. A short distance to her left ran a dirt road, and she could see a culvert beneath it that allowed for drainage. She thought that if she could reach that culvert, she might have protection should the bombs come again.

With great effort, and feeling terrible pain, she rolled over and over until she bumped her back hard against the embankment. Waves of pain ran through her bruised and burnt body. She felt quite strange now. In another moment, she felt nauseous and the landscape began to spin before her eyes. She closed her eyes tight, and in the darkness, she saw the ball of flame again, and she recalled all the horror.

She had run toward home, screaming. And then the wind came and she lay on the ground watching the house burn. She saw her baby brother, Billy, running and his clothes were on fire. She thought to help him and had managed to get shakily onto her feet when the wind came again. She recalled the last words her mother, who was in town at the time of the bombs falling, had told her. She had said, "God is good, and we are safe."

They had known for some time that a war was very likely. In the last days, when tension between the great powers were at a feverish pitch, there had been the praying in the large cathedral in town. And at night, the singing during the candle light vigils in the town square. She remembered how the candles had glowed bright-golden in the darkness, and how a euphoric feeling of hope, and one of peace, had washed over her. She had felt that the candles were beacons, lighthouses among the hatred, greed - - the madness that was engulfing the world. But too few had gathered.

The voices of the people rang in her head now. "A--maz-ing Grace, how sweet the sound, that saved a soul like me! I once was lost, but now am found; was blind, but now I see." Her little brother, Billy, had squeezed her hand and said, "I love you, Mary. No matter what happens, I will always love you."

Before the war, someone had been talking about the starving millions. A manned space ship sat burning on Mars. Global warming had brought about conditions that were resulting in the loss of much life.

And now it was over, finished. The soldiers were gone. All the flowers were gone. All the birds were gone.

Something was striking her body and she tried to shrink from the pain that the hits induced. Then she realized that it was raining. Washing the earth, she thought. Washing away our sins. She lay back on the parched earth. The rain drops stung her burned face, but they felt cool. Then the rain came hard and she had to turn her face away.

After several minutes, the rain slackened to a light drizzle, and suddenly, she felt cold and began to shiver. Turning and finding the culvert, she painfully dug her forearms into the parched earth until she dragged her body inside. Struggling, she turned her body in the cramped quarters, determined to face the outside air. Moments later, she lost consciousness.

When she awoke, it was dark. She hurt badly inside her body and her head hurt. She lay on her back with her arm beneath her head, supporting it. From the opening, she could see many stars, bright and looking as though they were close enough that she could reach out and touch one.

All of them suns, she thought. Perhaps some of them surrounded by planets much like earth. Inhabited by some form of life. She wondered if there could possibly be intelligent life out there, as on earth.

Now she laughed at that thought. A bitter, hysterical little laugh, and it sounded strange to her there in the culvert, in her tunnel, her tomb.

An intelligent form of life would never destroy itself, she thought. She laughed again and suddenly she was crying.

She thought of her dad now. Of their trips together, backpacking and mountain climbing. He had taught her to be strong, to be a survivor. But this time, she knew the odds were stacked against her.

Her father had died of cancer a year earlier. Now she was glad that he had passed away when he did, and so was spared having to see his family die and him unable to help them.

After a while, she slept, and when she awoke, it was dawn. The golden rays of the sun spot-lighted the scorched landscape. She felt terrible and smelled of decaying flesh and knew that she was going to die.

Without first thinking of doing so, she turned around in the small confines of the culvert and began crawling toward the far end of the tunnel. She crawled with her head down, her body racked by intense pain. She stopped only inches short of the clearing and buried her head in her arms as waves of dizziness ran before her eyes. After several minutes, she looked up and was surprised and delighted to see a lone, golden daffodil standing proud and tall in the first rays of sunlight. Protected from the death storm that had raged earlier by an earthen embankment on a concrete culvert.

"Little flower," she spoke aloud. "Little flower alone like me. How beautiful you are."

And reaching out, she touched it ever so gently and smiled for the first time in three days. And then she closed her eyes.

THE AWAKENING

Vanessa opened her eyes to the sharp cry of a seagull. She watched his sleek white body dive into the swift brown water and come up with a small fish.

"So . . . Where is God, little seagull?' she spoke aloud, her words sounding strange in the quietness of her surroundings.

"Can you fly to him, up there in the sky?"

Than a whisper, or perhaps it was merely a thought, but softly and clearly came back to her, "God lives in your heart."

She nodded her head, then thought without speaking. "Yes, but where was God when so many people were being butchered in Rwanda? Did God not also live in the hearts of those who were targeted for death?"

Yet, intuitively she knew. God was with the Tutsi Tribe, but the Tutsi didn't have that realization. And so, they did not place a mantle of protection around themselves through prayer. The Tutis had spent many years mistreating members of the Huta Tribe, until finally, the Hutu rose up in anger and hatred. Always, there are consequences to one's actions.

Neither tribe recognized that God is the life force within them. Within all of them. Within each one of us. That love and respect for one another was the answer to their problems.

Vanessa placed her feet in the cold, rushing water and it felt wonderful.

"If people are hungry and hurting and no one cares - - then love has gone," she thought. "If love dies, hope dies, God dies, we all die."

She looked into the cloudless blue sky and whispered ever so softly. "What is the last dream?"

And the message came back. "It is to have a world at peace. And you accomplish this by repeating silently to everyone you meet, I love you."

The End